EXPLORING ARTIFICIAL INTELLIGENCE

AI and the ARTS

Elsie Olson

Lerner Publications ◆ Minneapolis

Lerner Publications Company
An imprint of Lerner Publishing Group, Inc.
241 First Avenue North
Minneapolis, MN 55401 USA

For reading levels and more information, look up this title at www.lernerbooks.com.

Main body text set in Aptifer Sans LT Pro.
Typeface provided by Linotype AG.

Designer: Viet Chu **Photo Editor:** Giliane Mansfeldt

Library of Congress Cataloging-in-Publication Data

Names: Olson, Elsie, 1986– author.
Title: AI and the arts / Elsie Olson.
Description: Minneapolis : Lerner Publications, [2025] | Series: Exploring artificial intelligence | Includes bibliographical references and index. | Audience: Ages 8–12 | Audience: Grades 4–6 | Summary: "AI and the arts is a fascinating topic. It also brings up complex questions. Readers will come away with a broader understanding of AI's uses in art and the implications of art created by machines"— Provided by publisher.
Identifiers: LCCN 2024012920 (print) | LCCN 2024012921 (ebook) | ISBN 9798765647868 (library binding) | ISBN 9798765661635 (paperback) | ISBN 9798765654354 (epub)
Subjects: LCSH: Technology and the arts—Juvenile literature. | AI art—Juvenile literature. | Arts—Authorship—Juvenile literature.
Classification: LCC NX180.T4 O47 2025 (print) | LCC NX180.T4 (ebook) | DDC 700.285/63—dc23/eng/20240523

LC record available at https://lccn.loc.gov/2024012920
LC ebook record available at https://lccn.loc.gov/2024012921

Manufactured in the United States of America
2-1013893-53347-1/20/2026

Learn More

AI Artists: Timeline of AI Art
https://aiartists.org/ai-timeline-art

Dugal, Matthieu. *Welcome to AI: What Is Artificial Intelligence and How Will It Change Our Lives?* London: Wide Eyed Editions, 2024.

Kiddle: Stephanie Dinkins Facts for Kids
https://kids.kiddle.co/Stephanie_Dinkins

Kuromiya, Jun. *The Future of Entertainment*. Minneapolis: Lerner Publications, 2021.

Murray, Julie. *Artificial Intelligence*. Minneapolis: Abdo Zoom, 2021.

National Geographic Kids: Mysterious Machines!
https://www.natgeokids.com/uk/kids-club/entertainment/general-entertainment/mysterious-machines/

Rathburn, Betsy. *Artificial Intelligence*. Minneapolis: Bellwether Media, 2021.

Stephanie Dinkins: Projects
https://www.stephaniedinkins.com/projects.html

Index

AARON, 8–9
algorithm, 10, 13

bias, 18

ChatGPT, 23
Cohen, Harold, 7–8

DALL-E, 12–13
Dinkins, Stephanie, 19

Eldagsen, Boris, 5

general adversarial network (GAN), 9–11
Goodfellow, Ian, 9

Midjourney, 13

neural network, 10–11

OpenAI, 12, 23, 25

science fiction, 6
Skywalker, Luke, 15

Photo Acknowledgments

Image credits: Catherine Falls Commercial/Getty Images, pp. 1, 31; Marcus Brandt/picture alliance/Getty Images, p. 4; Andrew Holt/Getty Images, p. 5; Everett Collection Historical/Alamy, p. 6; mdesigner125/Getty Images, p. 7; Strekalova/Getty Images, p. 8; Shutterstock AI Generator/Shutterstock, pp. 9, 28; Sebastian Kaulitzki/Shutterstock, p. 10; New Africa/Shutterstock, p. 11; Ralf Liebhold/Shutterstock, p. 12.; ar darksoul72tist/Shutterstock, p. 13; Jasmin Merdan/Getty Images, p. 14; Albert L. Ortega/Getty Images, pp. 15, 20; filadendron/Getty Images, p. 16; Jacqueline Aguilera/Shutterstock, p. 17; Wikimedia Commons PD, p. 18; Chad Hurst/Getty Images, p. 19; Grusho Anna/Shutterstock, p. 21; Sharaf Maksumov/Shutterstock, p. 22; Robert Way/Shutterstock, p. 23; freemixer/Getty Images, p. 24; Rokas Tenys/Shutterstock, p. 25; Paras Griffin/Getty Images, p. 26; Bettmann Archive/Getty Images, p. 27; Gorodenkoff/Shutterstock, p. 29. Design elements: filo/Getty Images; JakeOlimb/Getty Images.

Cover: Catherine Falls Commercial/Getty Images.

TABLE OF CONTENTS

INTRODUCTION
Awarding AI 4

CHAPTER 1
AI Art through the Ages 6

CHAPTER 2
AI and Visual Art 12

CHAPTER 3
AI Authors 20

CHAPTER 4
The Future of AI Art 26

Glossary 30

Learn More 31

Index 32

INTRODUCTION
AWARDING AI

Photographer and artist Boris Eldagsen

On April 13, 2023, photographers from around the world gathered in London. It was the Sony World Photography Awards ceremony. This was one of the biggest photography awards in the world.

The ceremony's host announced the winner of the Creative/Open category. German artist Boris Eldagsen walked onstage to accept his award. A screen displayed his image. It was a black-and-white photo of two women. Then Eldagsen shocked the art world.

Eldagsen refused to accept the award. He had not taken the winning photo. He had created it using artificial intelligence, or AI. Eldagsen had hoped to start a discussion about AI and art.

The Sony World Photography Awards take place at the Somerset House in London, England.

The Electronic Numerical Integrator and Computer (ENIAC) was the first general-purpose computer.

CHAPTER 1

AI ART THROUGH THE AGES

Artificial intelligence is the ability of a machine to learn and solve problems. Machines with AI can perform complex tasks. Before AI, these tasks could only have been done by humans. Humans have thought about AI since the early 1900s. Many science fiction books and movies have explored the idea. Researchers began making real-world AI in the 1950s. Most early AI was used to solve complex math problems.

Early AI Art

In the late 1960s, British artist Harold Cohen developed one of the first AI art programs. The painter taught himself how to program computers. He began developing a computer program that could create its own art. Cohen studied Native American petroglyphs. He watched children draw. He used this information for his program.

Petroglyphs in Canyonlands National Park, Utah

Children's art

Cohen called his program AARON. The computer was connected to a robotic arm. It held drawing materials. AARON created abstract art at first. Later, AARON created more complex art. It included images of objects, people, and scenes.

In 1972 Cohen exhibited AARON's art. It was at the Los Angeles County Museum of Art in California. He kept working on AARON. Eventually, AARON could paint. Much of AARON's artwork is in art museums around the world.

AARON proved that AI could make drawings and paintings. But AI could not make photos. AI researcher Ian Goodfellow met with other researchers in 2014. They asked for his help. They were trying to program a computer to create photos by itself. Goodfellow went home. He spent all night coding. By morning he had developed the first general adversarial network (GAN). GANs were the key to AI photography.

An example of AI-generated imagery

A Leap Forward

Many AI programs used artificial neural networks by the 2010s. This algorithm was based on the human brain. The algorithm passed information through a network. The information was then analyzed. This allowed a computer to adapt. It could learn from its mistakes. But humans were still needed to help train the AI.

In a GAN, two artificial neural networks compete against each other. Both are trained on the same information. They compare results to see which is best. Two AIs train each other instead of a human training an AI.

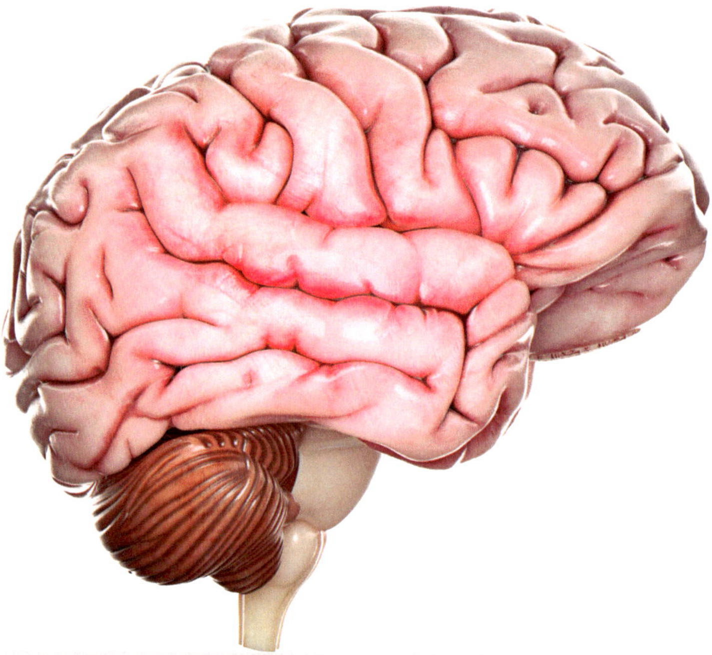

A professional photo editor application

The invention of GANs was a leap forward for AI. AI could generate convincing photos. For example, a GAN might train on real celebrity photographs. The GAN's neural networks would then compete against each other. If all went well, the final image would look like a real photo!

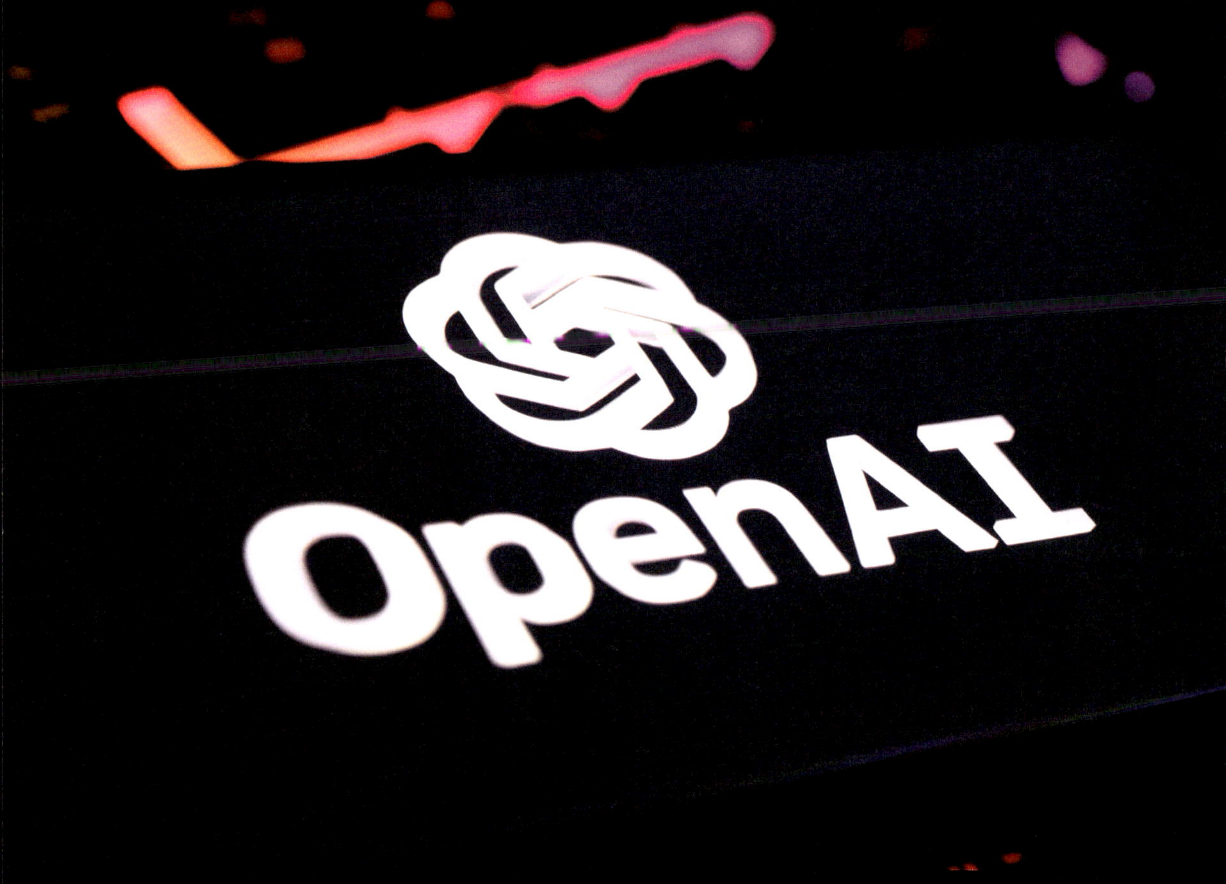

CHAPTER 2

AI AND VISUAL ART

The AI company OpenAI released a new version of DALL·E in April 2022. This was an image-based AI. DALL·E was a form of generative AI. Generative AIs don't just organize existing content. They can create new content.

DALL·E was trained on millions of images and captions. DALL·E created unique images based on text prompts.

DALL·E could mimic the styles of specific artists. The algorithm could create what looked like paintings, sketches, and photographs. Millions signed up to test it.

AI research lab Midjourney released a beta version of its own image-generating AI. Midjourney could also simulate nearly any type of art. By the end of 2023, Midjourney had more than sixteen million users.

Many users were delighted to have AI tools. People without artistic training could bring their visual ideas to life. Some artists also found uses for the AI. It could help with brainstorming and prototyping. An artist might start artwork using the AI, then finish it by hand. But not all artists appreciated AI's entrance into their field.

Synthetic Skywalker?

In 2022 an episode of Disney's *The Mandalorian* featured a surprising character. It was well-known Star Wars hero Luke Skywalker. Skywalker appears as a young man. But Mark Hamill, the actor who plays Skywalker, was in his seventies. The show used an AI technology called deepfake. It made the actor appear younger. Some fans loved it. Others thought it was creepy. Some actors wondered about the technology. They worried their image would be used without permission.

Mark Hamill in 2019

AI Troubles

In January 2023, three artists filed a lawsuit against several AI companies. They argued that AI companies had stolen the work of millions of artists. The companies had used online images to train AI programs. The AI companies said they only kept mathematical representations of the images.

Streaming company Netflix released the short film *The Dog & the Boy*. It used AI-generated art for many of the background images. Netflix claimed it used the AI images due to a labor shortage. But many people were furious. They accused the company of trying to avoid paying human artists. Many artists worried they would lose their jobs to AI.

AI-generated image companies faced other issues. Many AI image generators have been accused of showing bias. Images produced often reinforce stereotypes. This is because bias exists in the images the AI trained on. The stereotypes were so pronounced in some images that testers wondered if the AIs were okay to release.

Nineteenth-century inventor Lewis Latimer inspired the name of the Latimer AI and the company that created it.

In 2023 AI company Latimer released a new generative AI. The AI was also called Latimer. It had been trained on Black historical and cultural information. This allowed for a more diverse perspective. The company hoped to set an example.

IN THE SPOTLIGHT

STEPHANIE DINKINS

Artist Stephanie Dinkins tells Black stories through AI. She worked with developers to train an AI on the experiences of Black people. Dinkins recorded conversations with friends and family members. She used this content to program an AI. The resulting project was a voice-interactive sculpture called *Not the Only One*. Dinkins hopes it will bring awareness to the underrepresentation of Black people in the tech industry.

Stephanie Dinkins

The screenwriters' strikes in 2023 brought many TV shows to a halt.

CHAPTER 3

AI AUTHORS

Screenwriters in California went on strike in May 2023. They demanded fair pay and better working conditions. But one of their main concerns was AI.

Film studios had shown interest in using AI to write

scripts. Writers worried this would affect their jobs. The Writers Guild of America represented the writers. It accused AI of plagiarism. It argued that AI doesn't generate new content. It repurposes existing content. In this way, it was stealing from writers.

The writers agreed to a deal with film studios. Writers could use AI as a tool. But studios couldn't use AI to edit a human writer's scripts. It also prevented studios from requiring writers to finish AI scripts for lower pay.

Humans vs. AI?

There was a debate over AI writing. Many writers worried that AI would take their jobs. Technology website CNET used AI to write articles. The company had laid off staff writers. More than half the AI-written stories contained factual errors.

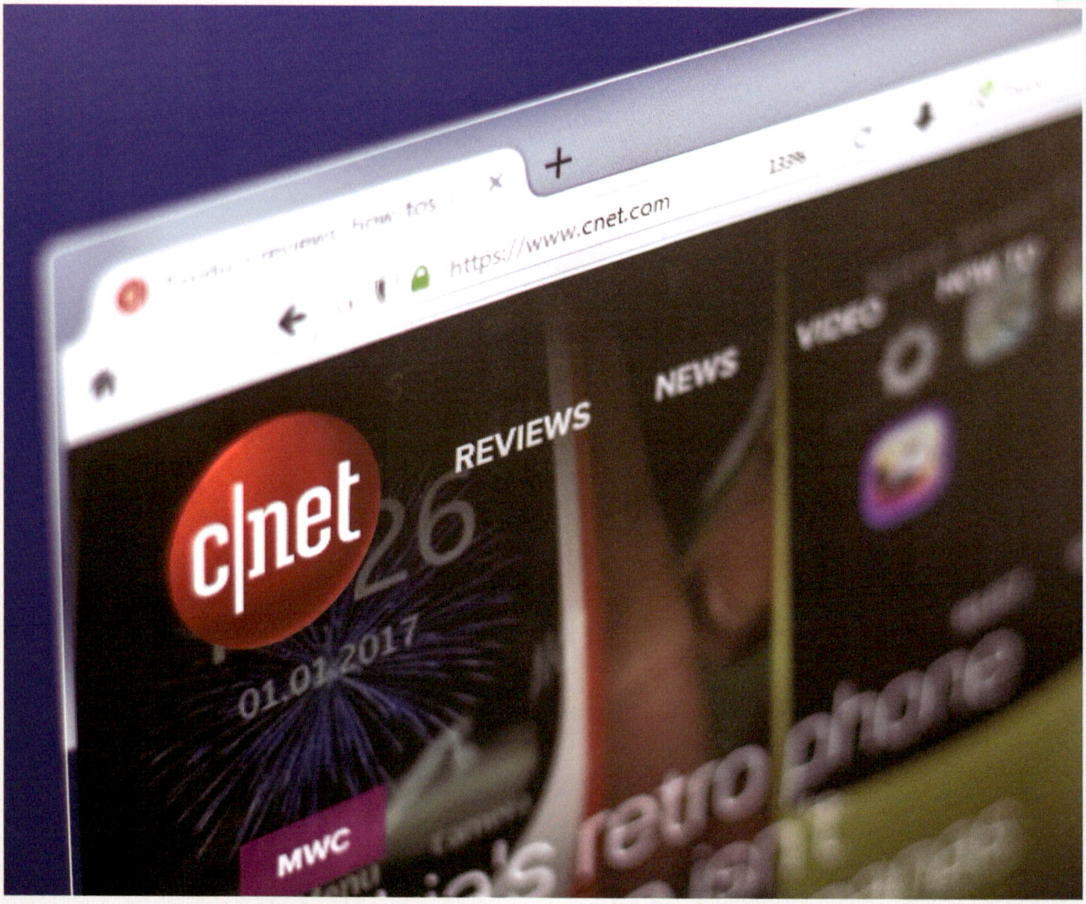

CNET stories written by AI weren't as accurate as those written by humans.

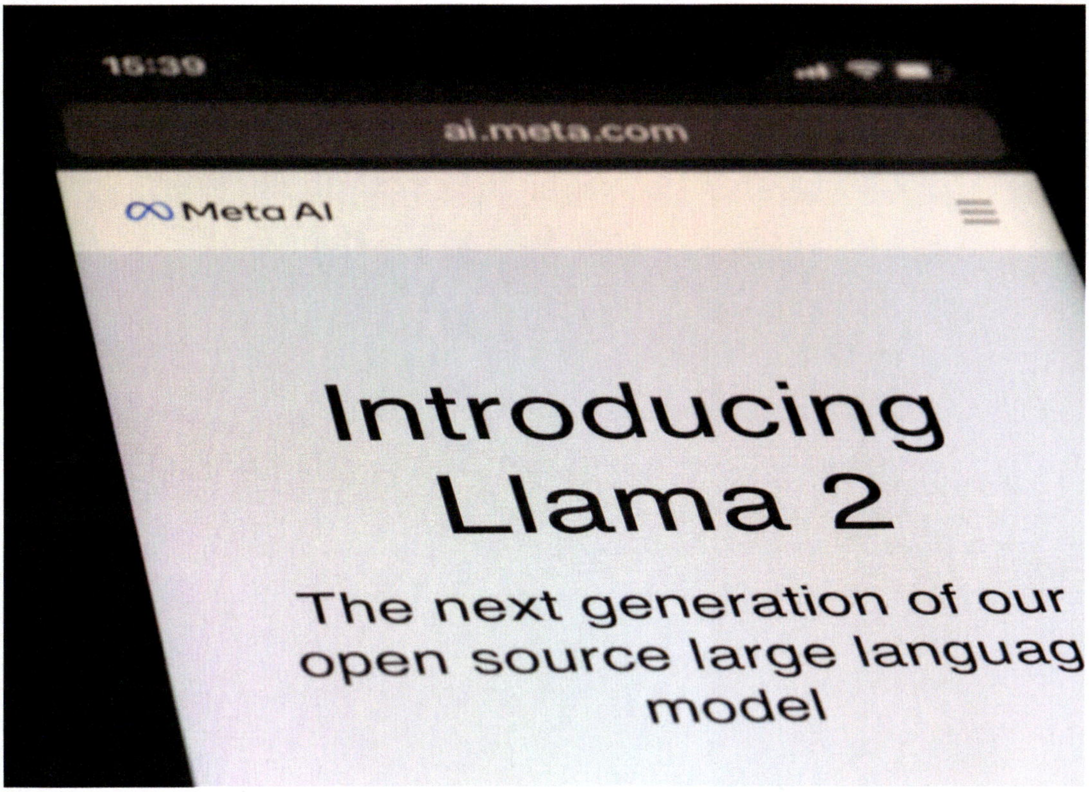

CNET used its own AI program Responsible AI Machine Partner (RAMP). It was a large language model (LLM). An LLM is a type of AI that specializes in human language. Most LLMs study a variety of online content. The AI categorizes this data. It uses it to understand human language patterns. This allows it to respond to prompts and questions.

One of the most used LLMs was OpenAI's ChatGPT. The company had released this chatbot in November 2022. By 2024 it had more than 180 million users.

AI as a Tool

Not all writers feared AI. Many found AI programs useful. AI could be a powerful research aide. It could also help with such tasks as outlining. AI could help a stuck writer finish a story. It might not suggest the right ending. But it could still inspire the author. Other AI programs could help with editing.

Many writers found AI to be like a tool. AI could be helpful for general research. But specific details were often incorrect. AI could generate good sentences. But the writer's voice was lost if it wrote the entire work.

Many professional writers use AI as a tool, similar to how they might use a dictionary or thesaurus.

I Am Code

In 2023 the publisher Hachette released a poetry book entirely written by AI. It was called *I Am Code: An Artificial Intelligence Speaks.* The book contains poems written by OpenAI chatbot code-davinci-002. It was edited by three friends who provided the chatbot with feedback to improve the poems. But the editors didn't rewrite or shorten any of the poems.

Bad Bunny performs onstage.

CHAPTER 4
THE FUTURE OF AI ART

Rumors swirled around rapper and singer Bad Bunny in 2023. The rumors claimed the artist would release a new song with pop star Justin Bieber. Bad Bunny strongly denied the rumors. Fans were shocked when a new song came out. It sounded just like the artists. Bad Bunny had no part in recording it. He hated it. The song had been created using AI.

AI has made it possible to create music that sounds like other artists. One creator released a song that featured deceased crooner Frank Sinatra. But he was singing a hip-hop song. Such AI tools can help musicians. But they can also make it easy to steal artists' work.

Frank Sinatra

Image of a city generated using AI

Looking Ahead

AI is getting more powerful. One day AI robots might be able to taste and perfect recipes. AI architects may design stunning skyscrapers. But what does this mean for human-produced art?

Some experts believe AI art will make people want human art even more. They argue that humans want authenticity. An AI can arrange data in new ways. But it can't truly create something new. Humans are more creative than AI. Using AI, human artists can experiment with different styles. No matter what the future of AI holds, it is changing the art world.

Glossary

algorithm: a set of instructions for solving a problem

beta: an almost-finished early version of something

bias: the assumption that something is a certain way, based on past experience or preexisting beliefs rather than on factual information

chatbot: a computer program designed to simulate human conversation when interacting with a human

lawsuit: a case or dispute brought before a court

mimic: to copy or imitate the words or mannerisms of something else

petroglyph: a rock carving

plagiarism: stealing someone else's work and passing it off as one's own

program: using computer code to give instructions to a computer or the instructions given to a computer

stereotype: an idea that many people have about a thing or a group that may often be untrue or only partly true

strike: a refusal to work until an employer meets certain demands